Chapter 1: Introduction to VBA – Why You Need It!

Introduction: Why You Need Excel VBA & How This Book Will Help You

Welcome to **Excel VBA for Absolute Beginners: Master Macros & Automation in Just 7 Days!** If you've ever found yourself performing the same tasks over and over in Excel—copying and pasting data, formatting reports, sending emails manually, or clicking through hundreds of cells—then this book is for you.

Imagine cutting your Excel workload in half with just a few lines of code! That's the power of **Visual Basic for Applications (VBA)**, the hidden gem inside Microsoft Excel that allows you to automate almost anything. Whether you're a **student, office worker, financial analyst, or business professional**, learning VBA will **save you time, eliminate repetitive tasks, and make you more valuable in your job**.

What is VBA, and Why Should You Learn It?

VBA (Visual Basic for Applications) is a programming language built into Excel that lets you automate tasks and create custom functions. Unlike standard Excel formulas, which work within individual cells, VBA allows you to control **entire spreadsheets, workbooks, and even other Microsoft Office applications** (like Word and Outlook).

Many people avoid learning VBA because they think programming is difficult. **But here's the secret: You don't need any prior coding experience to master VBA!** If you can use Excel, you can learn VBA with the right step-by-step approach—**and that's exactly what this book provides**.

Here are just a few things you'll be able to do with VBA after reading this book:

- **Automate repetitive Excel tasks** like formatting, data entry, and reporting
- **Write simple macros** to streamline your workflow
- **Create user-friendly forms** for data input
- **Generate and send emails automatically** from Excel
- **Eliminate manual errors** and make your work more efficient

Why This Book?

There are many Excel VBA books out there, so why choose this one? Unlike other VBA books that assume prior programming knowledge or overwhelm you with technical jargon, this book is **designed specifically for beginners**.

✓☐ **No coding experience required** – Everything is explained in plain English

✓☐ **Step-by-step learning** – Each chapter builds on the previous one for gradual progress

✓☐ **Hands-on exercises** – Learn by doing, with real-world examples you can apply immediately

✓☐ **Practical automation tips** – Save time at work and boost productivity

✓☐ **Troubleshooting tips** – Learn how to fix common errors and make your macros error-proof

How This Book is Structured

This book is designed as a **7-day learning plan**, where each chapter focuses on a key aspect of VBA:

> - **Day 1: Introduction to VBA & Setting Up Your Environment** – Getting comfortable with the VBA Editor
> - **Day 2: Recording and Editing Macros** – Learning how to create macros without writing a single line of code
> - **Day 3: VBA Fundamentals** – Understanding variables, loops, and conditions
> - **Day 4: Automating Common Excel Tasks** – Creating macros for data manipulation, formatting, and reports
> - **Day 5: Making Macros Interactive** – Adding user input and message boxes
> - **Day 6: Debugging & Error Handling** – Avoiding common mistakes and fixing issues
> - **Day 7: Real-World Projects** – Bringing it all together with practical automation

By the end of this book, you'll be **comfortable writing your own macros, automating tedious tasks, and improving your efficiency in Excel**.

Who is This Book For?

This book is perfect for:

- **Excel users** who want to automate tasks but have no programming experience
- **Office professionals** looking to work smarter and faster
- **Students and analysts** needing to process large amounts of data efficiently
- **Anyone who wants to learn a valuable skill** that will improve their job prospects

Ready to Get Started?

VBA might seem intimidating at first, but with **a little practice, you'll be automating tasks like a pro in no time!**

Turn the page, and let's begin your journey to **Excel VBA mastery!**

What is VBA and why it matters

The Hidden Power Inside Excel

If you've been using Microsoft Excel for a while, you've likely worked with formulas, charts, and maybe even PivotTables. But did you know that Excel has a **built-in programming language** that allows you to automate tasks, process large amounts of data, and even control other Office applications like Outlook and Word? This hidden power is called **Visual Basic for Applications (VBA)**.

VBA is a **scripting language** developed by Microsoft that allows users to **write macros**—small programs that automate repetitive tasks inside Excel. If you've ever recorded a macro before, you've already used VBA, even if you didn't realize it! However, recording macros is just the beginning. With VBA, you can go beyond simple automation and create **custom tools, complex data analysis solutions, and interactive applications** inside Excel.

Why Should You Care About VBA?

There are three major reasons why VBA is a valuable skill for any Excel user:

1. **Time-Saving   Automation**
   Think about how much time you spend on **repetitive tasks** in Excel—formatting reports, cleaning up data, copying and pasting values, or generating charts. With VBA, you can automate all of these tasks with a single click, **saving hours of manual work** every week.

2. **Increased   Accuracy   &   Consistency**
   Manual work leads to errors—especially when dealing with **large datasets**. A misplaced decimal, an accidental deletion, or forgetting to apply a formula correctly can cause serious mistakes. VBA ensures **precise and repeatable results**, reducing human errors and increasing efficiency.

3. **Powerful   Customization**
   Standard Excel functions are great, but sometimes you need **custom features** that aren't available in the built-in tools. With VBA, you can create personalized **functions, forms, and interactive dashboards** that go beyond Excel's default capabilities.

How VBA Fits Into the Bigger Picture

VBA is primarily used to automate Excel, but its power extends beyond just spreadsheets. It can also **control other Microsoft Office programs**, allowing you to:

✓ **Send automated emails from Excel** using Outlook
✓ **Generate Word reports** based on Excel data
✓ **Interact with Access databases** for advanced data management
✓ **Control PowerPoint presentations** directly from Excel

This makes VBA **a critical skill for professionals who work with data, reports, and large amounts of information across different software applications**.

But Isn't VBA Outdated?

You might have heard that newer technologies like Python or Power Automate are taking over VBA. While it's true that there are more automation tools available today, **VBA is still widely used in businesses, finance, and data analysis** because:

- **It's built into Excel**, meaning no extra software installation is required.

- **Companies rely on legacy VBA solutions**, making VBA skills highly valuable in the job market.

- **It's beginner-friendly**—unlike full programming languages like Python, you don't need to set up a coding environment to start automating tasks with VBA.

In short, VBA **isn't going anywhere anytime soon**—and learning it will instantly boost your productivity in Excel.

What's Next?

Now that you understand what VBA is and why it's important, let's dive into the **real benefits of Excel automation** in the next section. You'll learn how VBA can transform the way you work, **making Excel work for you instead of the other way around!**

Benefits of automating Excel tasks

If you use Excel regularly, you probably spend a lot of time repeating the same steps over and over: formatting reports, copying data, filtering tables, and creating charts. What if you could **eliminate these repetitive tasks and make Excel work for you**? That's exactly what **VBA (Visual Basic for Applications)** allows you to do.

By learning to automate tasks with VBA, you can **save time, reduce errors, and increase productivity**. Here's why **Excel automation** is a game-changer.

---

1. Save Hours of Work with a Single Click

Time is your most valuable asset—and automating Excel tasks with VBA can help you reclaim it.

Think about these common Excel tasks:

- Copying and pasting data between multiple sheets

- Formatting reports for weekly or monthly updates

- Applying formulas to hundreds or thousands of rows

- Filtering and sorting large datasets

- Generating PDF reports and emailing them manually

Each of these tasks might take **minutes or even hours** to complete manually. But with a VBA macro, you can automate them **in seconds**.

> ➤ **Example:** A financial analyst spends 2 hours every Friday creating a sales report by filtering data, formatting tables, and emailing results. With VBA, the same task can be **fully automated and completed in under 10 seconds**.

2. Eliminate Human Errors and Improve Accuracy

Manual data entry and repetitive Excel tasks **increase the risk of mistakes**. A simple typo, a misplaced formula, or forgetting to update a field can lead to serious errors—especially in financial reports or large datasets.

VBA ensures **consistency and accuracy** because macros follow **precise instructions** every time they run. Once a macro is set up correctly, it will always execute the same way, reducing the risk of human errors.

> **Example:** An accountant accidentally **deletes a column of numbers** while preparing a budget report. A VBA macro could prevent this mistake by automating the process, ensuring data integrity every time the report is generated.

3. Boost Productivity and Focus on High-Value Work

Repetitive Excel tasks **consume valuable time that could be spent on more important work**. Instead of manually sorting data or formatting tables, automation allows you to focus on:

- Analyzing trends and making better business decisions
- Improving workflows and optimizing processes
- Creating reports and dashboards that add real value

By reducing the time spent on **mundane Excel operations**, VBA allows you to be **more efficient and productive** in your daily work.

> **Example:** A project manager spends an hour every day updating project timelines in Excel. With a VBA macro, this task is **fully automated**, freeing up valuable time to focus on strategy and planning.

4. Simplify Complex Excel Operations

Excel is packed with features, but **some operations can be time-consuming or require complex formulas**. VBA simplifies these tasks by:

- Performing calculations that Excel formulas cannot handle

- Automating conditional formatting across multiple sheets

- Running advanced data analysis without requiring manual input

- Combining data from multiple files into a single report

> **Example:** A marketing team needs to compile sales data from **50 different Excel files** into one master sheet. Instead of manually opening each file, a VBA macro can **extract and consolidate the data in seconds**.

5. Automate Reports, Emails, and Notifications

One of the most powerful VBA applications is **automating emails and report distribution**. Instead of manually attaching reports to an email and sending them to your boss or team, VBA can do it for you.

You can set up VBA to:

- **Send automatic emails from Excel** (e.g., sales reports, performance updates)
- **Generate and save reports as PDFs** at scheduled times
- **Trigger reminders and notifications** based on deadlines or data changes
- ➤ **Example:** A company sends **daily sales reports** to regional managers. Instead of manually compiling and emailing these reports, a VBA macro automatically **extracts the data, formats the report, converts it to PDF, and sends it via Outlook—all in seconds.**

6. Make Your Work More Enjoyable

Let's face it—**nobody enjoys doing the same repetitive Excel tasks every day**. Manually entering data, applying filters, and formatting tables is tedious and exhausting. VBA eliminates boring, repetitive work and allows you to focus on **more interesting and strategic tasks**.

Instead of being an **Excel operator**, VBA turns you into an **Excel power user**. By automating tedious tasks, you can:

✓ **Reduce stress and frustration**

✓ **Speed up daily workflows**

✓ **Impress your colleagues and boss with your efficiency**

Final Thoughts: Why You Should Start Automating Today

VBA **isn't just a tool—it's a career-boosting skill** that can make you more efficient, reduce errors, and free up time for high-value tasks. Whether you're a **beginner, business professional, or Excel enthusiast, learning VBA will give you an edge in your job and make you more productive.**

In the next section, we'll explore **real-world examples of how professionals and companies use VBA to streamline their work, save time, and increase efficiency.**

Real-world applications and success stories

Now that you understand the **power of VBA** and the **benefits of automating Excel tasks**, let's explore **how professionals and businesses are using VBA in real-world scenarios**. From finance to marketing, and from HR to project management, VBA is transforming the way people work with Excel.

Below, you'll find **practical applications** of VBA across different industries, along with **success stories** of professionals who have used Excel automation to boost productivity, reduce errors, and save time.

---

1. Finance & Accounting – Automating Financial Reports & Budgeting

Application:

- Automating monthly and yearly financial reports

- Consolidating data from multiple spreadsheets

- Automating tax calculations and invoice processing

- Sending **automated email reports** to managers and clients

Success   Story:
Mark, a Senior Accountant at a multinational company, spent 3 hours every Monday manually consolidating sales data from multiple regional offices into a single Excel report. After learning VBA, he created a macro that automated the process—reducing his reporting time from 3 hours to just 5 minutes!

Mark's VBA macro automatically pulled data from different files, updated formulas, formatted the report, and emailed it as a PDF to his boss—all with a single click.

Impact:
Saved over **100+ hours per year** on reporting tasks
Eliminated **manual errors in financial reports**
Allowed Mark to focus on **data analysis instead of repetitive work**

---

2. Human Resources – Automating Employee Records & Payroll

Application:

- Automating **salary calculations** and deductions

- Generating performance reports

- Managing employee leave and attendance records

- Creating customized payslips using VBA

Success   Story:
Lisa, an HR Manager at a mid-sized firm, used to manually update and track employee attendance, which took her at least 8 hours every month. After implementing VBA, she built an automation system that automatically updated attendance records, calculated overtime pay, and generated monthly reports.

Lisa's macro saved an entire day of work every month and reduced payroll calculation errors significantly.

Impact:
Time   saved: 8+   hours   per   month
Improved   accuracy: No   more   manual   miscalculations
Faster HR processes for salary and performance reviews

---

3. Sales & Marketing – Automating Lead Tracking & Report Generation

Application:

- Automating the **compilation of sales data**

- Sending **personalized emails** to clients from Excel

- Creating **automated dashboards** for tracking sales performance

- Automating social media reports

Success   Story:
David, a Sales Manager, struggled with tracking and analyzing customer data for his company's sales team. Every week, he manually created reports by copying and pasting numbers from various sales spreadsheets. This process was slow, prone to mistakes, and frustrating.

With VBA, he built an automated reporting tool that compiled data, formatted it, and generated a detailed dashboard—all in under a minute!

David's macro extracted sales data, analyzed trends, and produced easy-to-read charts and reports, allowing him to make faster, data-driven decisions.

Impact:
Weekly reporting time reduced from 4 hours to 10 minutes
Improved decision-making with real-time analytics
Increased sales team productivity

---

4. Project Management – Tracking Deadlines & Automating Task Allocation

Application:

- Automating project timelines in Excel

- Sending reminders for upcoming deadlines

- Creating Gantt charts using VBA macros

- Assigning tasks automatically based on priority

Success   **Story:**
Sarah, a project manager in a software company, handled multiple teams and projects. Keeping track of deadlines and progress updates manually in Excel was inefficient. She used VBA to create an automated task tracker that assigned deadlines, sent email reminders, and updated the project dashboard in real-time.

Her VBA-powered tracker ensured that all team members received automatic updates about project deadlines, improving collaboration and efficiency.

Impact:
Improved project tracking & deadline management
Fewer missed deadlines due to automatic reminders
Better workflow coordination across teams

---

5. Data Analysis & Business Intelligence – Cleaning & Processing Large Datasets

Application:

- Automating **data cleaning & validation**

- Running **customized data analysis scripts**

- Filtering large datasets without manual intervention

- Automating **Pivot Table generation**

Success   Story:
*Michael, a data analyst, spent hours cleaning raw data before analyzing trends. Manually removing duplicates, fixing formatting issues, and structuring the data took up a lot of his time. After learning VBA, he wrote a **data-cleaning macro** that handled these tasks instantly!*

*His VBA tool processed **10,000+ rows of data in seconds**, preparing it for analysis much faster than before.*

Impact:
Hours of manual data cleaning reduced to seconds
More accurate and structured data for analysis
Faster and more efficient business insights

Final Thoughts: VBA is a Game-Changer for Every Industry

As these real-world examples show, **VBA is not just a technical skill— it's a career-enhancing tool that saves time, reduces errors, and boosts productivity across multiple industries.**

Whether you work in **finance, HR, sales, project management, or data analysis**, knowing how to automate tasks in Excel with VBA **can make you more efficient and valuable in your organization.**

In the next section, we'll cover **how to use this book effectively** so you can start applying VBA to your own work and unlocking the full potential of Excel automation!

How to use this book effectively

Congratulations! You've taken the first step towards learning **Excel VBA and automation**—a skill that will save you time, boost your productivity, and help you work smarter. To get the most out of this book, follow the strategies below to ensure a smooth and effective learning experience.

---

1. Follow the Step-by-Step Learning Approach

This book is designed for **absolute beginners**, meaning you don't need any prior programming experience. **Each chapter builds on the previous one**, introducing concepts gradually to help you learn at your own pace.

Best way to approach this book:
✓ **Read in order** – The chapters are arranged to take you from beginner to proficient VBA user step by step.
✓ **Don't rush** – Practice each concept before moving on to the next.
✓ **Apply what you learn** – Use the exercises and examples in real-world Excel files.

---

2. Practice by Writing and Running Code Yourself

Reading about VBA is great, but **the best way to learn is by doing**. Instead of just copying and pasting code, type it manually to understand the syntax and structure.

Tips for hands-on practice:
✓ **Use a test Excel workbook** – Create a practice file where you can experiment without affecting important data.
✓ **Try modifying examples** – Change values, add new features, and see what happens.
✓ **Debug errors fearlessly** – Mistakes are part of learning. Use the built-in debugging tools to find and fix issues.

---

3. Use the Code Examples and Exercises

This book includes **real-world examples and ready-to-use VBA macros** to help you apply what you learn. Each chapter contains:

- **Code snippets** – Short VBA examples to illustrate key concepts.

- **Step-by-step tutorials** – Practical guides to help you build useful macros.
- **Exercises and challenges** – Tasks at the end of each chapter to reinforce learning.

How to get the most out of exercises:
✓ **Attempt them on your own first** before checking the solution.
✓ **Experiment with variations** – Try modifying the code to see different outcomes.
✓ **Keep notes** – Write down key learnings and challenges you faced.

---

4. Use Debugging Techniques to Solve Errors

As a beginner, you will **encounter errors** in your code—it's completely normal! Learning **how to debug and fix errors** is a crucial part of mastering VBA.

Debugging strategies in this book:
✓ **Understanding error messages** – Learn how to interpret and fix common errors.
✓ **Using breakpoints** – Stop your code at a specific point to inspect what's happening.
✓ **Testing small sections of code** – Run your macros in parts to identify mistakes.

When you make an error, don't get frustrated! Instead, see it as an opportunity to **understand how VBA works**. The more errors you debug, the better you'll become at writing efficient code.

---

5. Apply VBA to Real-World Tasks Immediately

The best way to retain what you learn is to **use VBA in your daily work**. Instead of just following the book's examples, think about how you can automate **your own Excel tasks**.

Ways to apply VBA immediately:
✓ Identify **repetitive tasks** in your daily Excel work (e.g., formatting, data entry).
✓ Create a **simple macro** to automate one of those tasks.
✓ Gradually improve your macros by **adding user input or logic**.
✓ Share your macros with colleagues to **increase productivity in your workplace**.

The sooner you start using VBA **on real tasks**, the faster you'll see its power in action.

---

6. Use Online Resources and VBA Communities

Even after finishing this book, you will continue learning. VBA is a **vast and evolving language**, and new challenges will arise as you automate more tasks. Luckily, there are **great online communities and resources** to help you when you get stuck.

Recommended   VBA   resources:
✓ **Microsoft's VBA Documentation** – The official reference guide.
✓ **Stack Overflow** – A great place to ask VBA-related questions.
✓ **Excel forums & YouTube tutorials** – Learn from other VBA users.
✓ **GitHub repositories** – Find and share VBA projects.

---

7. Be Patient and Have Fun!

Learning VBA **is like learning a new language**—it takes practice and patience. Don't worry if some concepts seem difficult at first. Over time, things will start to click, and you'll gain confidence in your ability to automate Excel tasks.

Final   motivation   tips:
✓ **Celebrate small wins** – Every working macro is a step forward.
✓ **Experiment freely** – Don't be afraid to try new things.
✓ **Enjoy the process** – Learning VBA is a **career-enhancing skill** that will make your work easier and more enjoyable.

Final Thoughts: Let's Start Automating!

By following this book's structured learning path, practicing the exercises, and applying VBA to your real-world Excel tasks, you'll become **proficient in Excel automation faster than you think**.

Now that you know **how to get the most out of this book**, it's time to **dive into VBA and start your journey to automation mastery**. Let's begin with **setting up your VBA environment in the next chapter!** 🪄

Chapter 2: Setting Up Your VBA Environment

Before we dive into writing VBA code, we need to **set up Excel properly**. By default, the tools required for VBA programming are hidden in Excel. In this chapter, we will:

✓ **Enable the Developer Tab** – This gives you access to the VBA editor and macro tools.

✓ **Navigate the VBA Editor (VBE)** – Learn how to use the interface where you write and manage your VBA code.

✓ **Write Your First Macro** – A simple "Hello, VBA!" program to get you started.

✓ **Run, Edit, and Delete Macros** – Learn how to execute, modify, and remove VBA code.

By the end of this chapter, you will be **comfortable working in the VBA environment** and ready to start automating Excel!

Enabling the Developer Tab in Excel

What is the Developer Tab?

The **Developer Tab** is a special section in the Excel ribbon that gives you access to **VBA tools, macros, ActiveX controls, and form elements**. Since it's hidden by default, we need to enable it before we can start writing VBA code.

How to Enable the Developer Tab

Follow these simple steps to **unlock the Developer Tab** in Excel:

1. Open Excel and go to Options

- Open **Microsoft Excel**.

- Click **File** in the top-left corner.

- Select **Options** (near the bottom).

2□. Access the Ribbon Customization Menu

- In the **Excel Options** window, click **Customize Ribbon** from the left panel.

3□. Enable the Developer Tab

- On the right side, look for **Main Tabs**.

- Find **Developer** and check the box next to it.

- Click **OK** to save your changes.

4□. Verify the Developer Tab is Visible

- Look at the Excel ribbon. You should now see a **Developer** tab next to the View tab.

- Click it, and you'll see **Macro, Visual Basic, Record Macro, and other VBA-related tools**.

Congratulations! You've enabled the Developer Tab and can now start working with VBA.

Navigating the VBA Editor (VBE)

What is the VBA Editor?

The **VBA Editor (VBE)** is where you **write, edit, and manage VBA code**. It's a separate interface inside Excel designed for coding.

To open the **VBA Editor**, use one of these methods:

- Click **Developer > Visual Basic** in the ribbon.
- Press **ALT + F11** (a faster shortcut).

Once inside, you'll see several **important components**:

Main Components of the VBA Editor

- **Project Explorer** – Shows all open Excel workbooks and sheets. Think of it as your file manager for VBA projects.
- **Code Window** – The main area where you write and edit VBA code.
- **Immediate Window** – A tool for testing and debugging code in real time.
- **Properties Window** – Displays properties of objects (such as worksheets or forms) that you can modify.

Customizing the VBA Editor for Easier Use

To make coding easier, enable some **useful settings**:

- Click **View > Immediate Window** (Ctrl + G) – This helps you test small VBA commands instantly.

- Click **View > Project Explorer** (Ctrl + R) – Always keep this visible to manage your VBA modules easily.

- Click **Tools > Options** – Here, you can adjust settings like **Auto Syntax Check** (turn it off to avoid annoying pop-ups).

Now, you're familiar with the VBA Editor interface and ready to write your first macro!

Writing your first simple macro (Hello, VBA!)

Now that we have everything set up, let's write our **first VBA macro**.

What is a Macro?

A **macro** is a recorded or written VBA script that automates a task in Excel. Macros **eliminate repetitive manual work** and run at the click of a button.

How to Write Your First Macro

Let's create a simple VBA program that **displays a message box saying "Hello, VBA!"**

1☐. **Open the VBA Editor**

- Press **ALT + F11** to open the VBA Editor.

2☐. **Insert a New Module**

- In the VBA Editor, click **Insert > Module.**

- A new blank code window appears. This is where you write your VBA code.

3☐. **Write the VBA Code**

- Copy and paste the following VBA script into the module:

```
Sub HelloVBA()
    MsgBox "Hello, VBA!", vbInformation, "My First Macro"
End Sub
```

4☐. **Understanding the Code**

- Sub HelloVBA() – This defines a macro named **HelloVBA.**

- MsgBox "Hello, VBA!", vbInformation, "My First Macro" – Displays a **message box** with the text "Hello, VBA!" and a title.

- End Sub – This marks the **end of the macro.**

Congratulations! You've written your first VBA program. Now, let's run it!

How to run, edit, and delete macros

Running a Macro

To run the macro you just created:

Method 1: From the VBA Editor

- In the VBA Editor, place your cursor inside the Sub HelloVBA() macro.

- Press **F5** (Run) or click **Run > Run Sub/UserForm**.

- A message box should appear, displaying "Hello, VBA!"

Method 2: From the Excel Macro Menu

- Close the VBA Editor (ALT + Q).

- Go to **Developer > Macros**.

- Select **HelloVBA** from the list.

- Click **Run**.

Editing a Macro

- Open the **VBA Editor (ALT + F11)**.

- Find your macro in the **Module** where you wrote it.

- Make changes to the code (e.g., modify the text inside MsgBox).

- Save the workbook to keep the changes.

Deleting a Macro

To remove a macro from your workbook:

1. Open the **VBA Editor (ALT + F11)**.

2. Locate the macro inside the **Module**.

3. Delete the code, or delete the entire **Module** (right-click > Remove Module).

Final Thoughts: You're Ready to Start Automating!

By now, you have:

- Enabled the **Developer Tab**
- Learned how to **navigate the VBA Editor**
- Written your **first simple macro**
- Learned how to **run, edit, and delete macros**

This is just the beginning! In the next chapters, we will dive deeper into **VBA programming**, where you'll learn how to **write more powerful macros, automate real-world Excel tasks, and customize Excel like a pro**.

Next up: Mastering the Macro Recorder – Automate Excel Without Coding!

Chapter 3: The Macro Recorder –
Your Secret Automation Weapon

Have you ever wished you could automate repetitive tasks in Excel **without writing a single line of code**? The **Macro Recorder** is your **secret weapon**! It allows you to **record your actions in Excel and convert them into VBA code**, making automation easy—even if you've never programmed before.

In this chapter, we will cover:

✓ **Recording and modifying macros without coding**
✓ **Automating simple formatting tasks**
✓ **Understanding how the Macro Recorder converts actions into VBA code**
✓ **Limitations of recorded macros (and how to improve them)**

By the end of this chapter, you'll be able to **create your first automation in Excel without touching code**, and then fine-tune it for even better results.

Recording and modifying macros without coding

What is the Macro Recorder?

The **Macro Recorder** is a built-in tool in Excel that allows you to **record** your actions—such as formatting, copying data, or applying formulas—and then **replay them automatically** whenever needed.

Think of it as Excel remembering everything you do and repeating it for you!

The best part? The Macro Recorder **automatically generates VBA code** behind the scenes, meaning you can use it even if you don't know programming.

How to Record a Macro in Excel

Let's record a **simple macro** that automatically formats a table with bold headers, yellow highlights, and borders.

Step 1: Open the Macro Recorder

1. Go to the **Developer Tab** (If you don't see it, refer to Chapter 2 on enabling it).

2. Click **Record Macro** (in the Code group).

Step 2: Name Your Macro

A window will appear asking you to name your macro.

- **Macro name:** FormatTable (use a name without spaces)

- **Shortcut key (optional):** Press **Ctrl + Shift + T** to assign a shortcut

- **Store macro in: This Workbook**

- Click **OK** to start recording.

Step 3: Perform the Actions You Want to Automate

Now, Excel is **recording everything you do!** Follow these steps:

1. **Select the table you want to format.**

2. **Make the headers bold** (Ctrl + B).

3. **Apply a yellow background** to the headers (**Home > Fill Color > Yellow**).

4. **Add borders** to the entire table (**Home > Borders > All Borders**).

Step 4: Stop Recording

Once done, go to **Developer > Stop Recording**.

Congratulations! You have just recorded your first macro.

Automating simple formatting tasks

How to Run the Macro You Just Recorded

Now that you've recorded a macro, you can **use it instantly** to format any table in one click!

Method 1: Using the Macros Menu

1. Go to **Developer > Macros**.

2. Select **FormatTable**.

3. Click **Run**—your formatting is instantly applied!

Method 2: Using a Keyboard Shortcut

If you assigned **Ctrl + Shift + T** as a shortcut earlier, just press it, and the formatting is done automatically.

Modifying a Recorded Macro

You can **edit your recorded macro** to make it better!

Opening the Macro Code

1. Press **ALT + F11** to open the **VBA Editor**.

2. Find your macro under **Modules > Module1**.

3. Double-click it to view the code.

Here's what the recorded macro might look like:

```
Sub FormatTable()
    ' Makes header bold
    Selection.Font.Bold = True
    ' Adds yellow background color
    Selection.Interior.Color = RGB(255, 255, 0)
    ' Adds borders
    Selection.Borders.LineStyle = xlContinuous
End Sub
```

Making Small Improvements

28

What if you want the macro to always format the first row as headers?

Modify the code like this:

```vba
Sub FormatTable()
    Range("A1:Z1").Font.Bold = True
    Range("A1:Z1").Interior.Color = RGB(255, 255, 0)
    Range("A1:Z20").Borders.LineStyle = xlContinuous
End Sub
```

Now, the macro will **always** format the headers in row 1 and apply borders to the first 20 rows!

Understanding how the Macro Recorder converts actions into VBA code

The Macro Recorder **translates** everything you do in Excel into **VBA commands**. This is a great way to learn how VBA works **without needing to code from scratch**.

Let's say you **bold a selection manually** while recording. The VBA code it generates might look like this:

```
Selection.Font.Bold = True
```

Every action has an equivalent VBA command! The more you record, the more you start understanding VBA syntax.

However, recorded macros **aren't perfect**—which leads us to the next section.

Limitations of recorded macros (and how to improve them)

While the Macro Recorder is a great starting point, it has **some limitations**:

1. Macros Work Only for the Exact Steps You Recorded

If you record a macro on **specific cells (e.g., A1:C5)**, it will **only** work on those cells. If your table grows, the macro won't adapt.

How to improve it: Use **dynamic ranges** instead of fixed cell references.

```
Sub FormatDynamicTable()
    Dim LastRow As Long
    LastRow = Cells(Rows.Count, 1).End(xlUp).Row   ' Find
last row in Column A
    Range("A1:Z" & LastRow).Borders.LineStyle =
xlContinuous
End Sub
```

This version automatically adjusts to the size of the table.

---

2. Macros Record Every Click, Even Unnecessary Ones

Recorded macros sometimes contain **extra, unnecessary steps**, making them inefficient.

How to improve it: Remove redundant lines in the VBA Editor.

Example of unnecessary recorded code:

```
Range("A1").Select
Selection.Font.Bold = True
```

Better version:

```
Range("A1").Font.Bold = True   ' Directly applies bold
without selecting
```

Avoid selecting cells unnecessarily—it speeds up macros!

3. Macros Can't Handle User Input

Recorded macros don't allow users to **enter values dynamically**.

How to improve it: Use InputBox to prompt the user for input.

```
Sub AskUser()
    Dim UserText As String
    UserText = InputBox("Enter a message:")
    MsgBox "You entered: " & UserText
End Sub
```

This allows interaction between the macro and the user!

Final Thoughts: You're Now an Excel Automation Expert!

Key Takeaways from This Chapter:

- The **Macro Recorder** lets you automate Excel **without coding**.
- Macros can be **run with a shortcut** or from the Macros menu.
- You can **edit recorded macros** in the VBA Editor to improve efficiency.
- Recorded macros have **limitations**, but small improvements can make them smarter and more flexible.

In the next chapter, we'll take things further and **start writing VBA code from scratch** to build powerful automation tools!

Next Up: Mastering VBA Programming Basics!

Chapter 4: VBA Programming Basics – No Coding Experience Needed!

Now that you've learned how to **record macros** and modify them, it's time to take your VBA skills to the next level by **writing your own VBA code from scratch**!

In this chapter, you'll learn the **fundamental building blocks** of VBA programming, including:

✓ **Understanding variables and data types** – Store and manipulate data in VBA.

✓ **Using If statements for decision-making** – Make your macros smarter.

✓ **Loops: Automating repetitive tasks** – Repeat actions automatically.

✓ **Debugging basics: Fixing errors in your macros** – Identify and correct issues in your code.

By the end of this chapter, you'll be able to **write VBA programs confidently and automate complex Excel tasks with ease!**

Understanding variables and data types

What Are Variables in VBA?

A **variable** is a container that holds **temporary** data in a macro. Think of a variable like a cell in Excel—it stores a value that can change while the program is running.

Declaring a Variable in VBA

Before using a variable, you need to **declare** it using the Dim keyword:

```
Dim EmployeeName As String

Dim Salary As Double

Dim Age As Integer
```

Common Data Types in VBA

Data Type Example Value Usage

String	"John Doe"	Text values (names, addresses)
Integer	25	Whole numbers (age, counts)
Double	2500.75	Decimal numbers (salary, percentage)
Boolean	True / False	Yes/No decisions
Date	#01/01/2024#	Date and time

Assigning Values to Variables

Once a variable is declared, you can assign it a value:

```
Dim Name As String

Name = "Alice"

MsgBox "Employee: " & Name
```

Pro Tip: Always use meaningful variable names so your code is easier to read!

Using If statements for decision-making

An **If statement** allows VBA to **make decisions** based on conditions.

For example, let's say we want to **check if an employee is eligible for a bonus** based on their sales:

```
Sub CheckBonus()
    Dim Sales As Double
    Sales = 5000 ' Example sales amount

    If Sales >= 5000 Then
        MsgBox "Congratulations! You earned a bonus!"
    Else
        MsgBox "Keep going! Reach $5000 to get a bonus."
    End If
End Sub
```

Adding Multiple Conditions (ElseIf)

You can add **multiple conditions** using ElseIf:

```
Sub CheckPerformance()
    Dim Score As Integer
    Score = 85 ' Example performance score

    If Score >= 90 Then
        MsgBox "Excellent Performance!"
    ElseIf Score >= 75 Then
        MsgBox "Good Job! Keep improving!"
    Else
        MsgBox "Needs Improvement. Keep working!"
    End If
End Sub
```

Use If statements to make your macros react differently based on user input or data values.

Loops: Automating repetitive tasks

What Are Loops?

A **loop** allows VBA to **repeat a task multiple times,** saving you from manually performing the same action over and over.

Example Use Case: You want to **highlight all negative numbers** in a large dataset—doing this manually would take forever!

Types of Loops in VBA

Loop Type	Purpose	Example Use Case
For Next	Loops a specific number of times	Formatting 100 rows of data
Do While	Loops while a condition is TRUE	Keep asking for input until valid data is entered
Do Until	Loops until a condition is TRUE	Repeat until a blank cell is found

Using a For Next Loop to Automate Formatting

Let's say you have **10 rows of data**, and you want to **make all text in column A bold** automatically. Instead of doing this manually, use a **loop:**

```
Sub BoldText()
    Dim i As Integer
    For i = 1 To 10 ' Loops from row 1 to 10
        Range("A" & i).Font.Bold = True
    Next i
End Sub
```

This **saves hours of work** when working with large datasets!

Using a Do While Loop to Process Data Until a Blank Cell Is Found

A **Do While** loop is useful when you don't know how many rows there are:

```vba
Sub HighlightNegativeNumbers()
    Dim i As Integer
    i = 1 ' Start at row 1


    Do While Cells(i, 2).Value <> "" ' Loop until an empty
cell is found
        If Cells(i, 2).Value < 0 Then
            Cells(i, 2).Interior.Color = RGB(255, 0, 0) '
Highlight in red
        End If
        i = i + 1 ' Move to the next row
    Loop
End Sub
```

Loops make Excel automation extremely powerful, saving you time on large tasks!

Debugging basics: Fixing errors in your macros

When writing VBA code, **errors happen—it's completely normal!**
Learning how to **debug and fix errors** is an important part of
becoming a VBA expert.

Common Types of Errors in VBA

Error Type	Cause	Example
Syntax Error	Typing mistake	MsgBox "Hello (Missing closing quote)
Runtime Error	Code tries to do something impossible	Dividing by zero
Logical Error	Code runs but gives incorrect results	Using wrong calculations

Using Debugging Tools to Fix Errors

1. Step Through Code (F8 Key)

Press **F8** in the **VBA Editor** to **execute your macro one line at a time.** This helps you find exactly where the error occurs.

2. Using the Immediate Window (Ctrl + G)

Test values in real-time by typing commands here.

Example:

```
? Range("A1").Value
```

Press **Enter** and it will display the value of A1!

3. Using Breakpoints (F9)

Breakpoints **pause the macro at a specific line,** allowing you to
inspect values before continuing execution.

Final Thoughts: You're Now a VBA Programmer!

Key Takeaways from This Chapter:

Variables store and manipulate data in VBA.
If statements allow VBA to **make decisions** based on conditions.
Loops let you **repeat tasks automatically** (saving time!).
Debugging helps you find and fix errors efficiently.

You are now writing real VBA code! With these basics, you can start creating **powerful automation scripts**.

Next up: Automating Real-World Excel Tasks with VBA!

Chapter 5: Automating Everyday Excel Tasks

Now that you understand **VBA programming basics**, it's time to **apply your skills to real-world Excel automation**. In this chapter, you'll learn how to:

✓ **Auto-format reports in seconds** – Make reports look professional with one click.

✓ **Send automated emails from Excel** – Email reports directly from VBA.

✓ **Copy and paste data between sheets dynamically** – Automate data consolidation.

✓ **Create simple dashboards with VBA** – Build interactive reports without manual effort.

By the end of this chapter, you'll be able to **automate common Excel tasks that take hours and complete them in seconds!**

Auto-formatting reports in seconds

Formatting reports manually—bolding headers, applying colors, adjusting column widths—can be **time-consuming** and **error-prone**. Let's write a **VBA macro to format a report automatically** in one click.

VBA Code: Auto-Format a Report

```vba
Sub FormatReport()
    Dim ws As Worksheet
    Set ws = ActiveSheet ' Apply formatting to the active
worksheet

    ' Bold headers in row 1
    ws.Rows(1).Font.Bold = True

    ' Apply yellow background to headers
    ws.Rows(1).Interior.Color = RGB(255, 255, 0)

    ' Auto-fit columns
    ws.Cells.EntireColumn.AutoFit

    ' Add borders to the entire data range
    Dim LastRow As Long
    LastRow = ws.Cells(Rows.Count, 1).End(xlUp).Row
    ws.Range("A1:Z" & LastRow).Borders.LineStyle =
xlContinuous

    MsgBox "Report formatting completed!", vbInformation,
"Success"
End Sub
```

How This Works:

✓ **Bolds the headers in row 1**
✓ **Applies a yellow background**

✓ **Auto-adjusts column width**
✓ **Adds borders to all data**

How to Use It:

1☐. Open your report.
2☐. Press **ALT + F11** to open the VBA Editor.
3☐. Paste the code into a module.
4☐. Run the macro (F5 or Developer > Macros > Run).

Your report is now formatted professionally in seconds!

Sending automated emails from Excel

You can use VBA to **send emails directly from Excel using Outlook**. This is useful for emailing reports, reminders, or bulk messages.

VBA Code: Send an Email from Excel

```
Sub SendEmail()
    Dim OutlookApp As Object
    Dim OutlookMail As Object
    Dim ws As Worksheet
    Set ws = ActiveSheet

    ' Create Outlook application and email
    Set OutlookApp = CreateObject("Outlook.Application")
    Set OutlookMail = OutlookApp.CreateItem(0)

    ' Email settings
    With OutlookMail
        .To = "recipient@example.com"
        .CC = ""
        .BCC = ""
        .Subject = "Automated Report"
        .Body = "Hello, attached is the latest report."
        .Attachments.Add ws.Parent.FullName ' Attach the
current workbook
        .Send ' Change to .Display if you want to preview
before sending
    End With

    ' Cleanup
    Set OutlookMail = Nothing
    Set OutlookApp = Nothing
```

43

```
    MsgBox "Email sent successfully!", vbInformation,
"Success"
End Sub
```

How This Works:

✓ **Creates an Outlook email**
✓ **Attaches the current workbook**
✓ **Sends the email automatically**

How to Use It:

1☐. Update the recipient's email address.
2☐. Run the macro (F5 in the VBA Editor).
3☐. Check your **Sent Items** in Outlook.

Your email is sent instantly without opening Outlook!

Copy-pasting data between sheets dynamically

If you regularly **copy and paste data** between sheets, you can **automate** this task with VBA.

VBA Code: Copy Data from One Sheet to Another

```
Sub CopyData()
    Dim wsSource As Worksheet, wsTarget As Worksheet
    Dim LastRow As Long

    ' Define source and target sheets
    Set wsSource = ThisWorkbook.Sheets("Sheet1")
    Set wsTarget = ThisWorkbook.Sheets("Sheet2")

    ' Find last used row in source sheet
    LastRow = wsSource.Cells(Rows.Count, 1).End(xlUp).Row

    ' Copy data from source to target
    wsSource.Range("A1:Z" & LastRow).Copy
    wsTarget.Range("A1").PasteSpecial Paste:=xlPasteValues

    ' Clean up clipboard
    Application.CutCopyMode = False

    MsgBox "Data copied successfully!", vbInformation,
"Success"
End Sub
```

How This Works:

✓ **Finds the last row with data** in Sheet1
✓ **Copies all data to Sheet2**
✓ **Pastes only values to remove formulas**

45

How to Use It:

1☐. Replace "Sheet1" and "Sheet2" with your actual sheet names.
2☐. Run the macro (F5 in the VBA Editor).

Your data is copied instantly without errors!

Creating simple dashboards with VBA

Dashboards **summarize data visually** using charts, tables, and buttons. VBA can automate dashboard creation, making updates quick and dynamic.

VBA Code: Create a Simple Dashboard with a Button

```
Sub CreateDashboard()
    Dim ws As Worksheet
    Set ws = ThisWorkbook.Sheets.Add
    ws.Name = "Dashboard"

    ' Add a title
    ws.Range("A1").Value = "Sales Dashboard"
    ws.Range("A1").Font.Size = 16
    ws.Range("A1").Font.Bold = True

    ' Insert a chart
    Dim ChartObj As ChartObject
    Set ChartObj = ws.ChartObjects.Add(Left:=100, Top:=50, Width:=400, Height:=250)
    With ChartObj.Chart
        .SetSourceData Source:=ThisWorkbook.Sheets("SalesData").Range("A1:B10")
        .ChartType = xlColumnClustered
        .HasTitle = True
        .ChartTitle.Text = "Sales Performance"
    End With

    MsgBox "Dashboard created!", vbInformation, "Success"
End Sub
```

How This Works:

✓ Creates a new worksheet for the dashboard
✓ Adds a title
✓ Inserts a chart using sales data

How to Use It:

1☐. Ensure you have a sheet named "SalesData" with data in A1:B10.
2☐. Run the macro (F5 in the VBA Editor).

Your interactive dashboard is generated automatically!

Final Thoughts: Excel Automation Made Easy!

Key Takeaways from This Chapter:

Auto-format reports to make them look professional in seconds.
Send automated emails from Excel without opening Outlook.
Copy and paste data dynamically between sheets.
Create simple dashboards with VBA for real-time reporting.

You now have the power to automate daily Excel tasks effortlessly!

Next up: Making Your Macros Interactive – Adding User Inputs & Forms!

Chapter 6: Making Your Macros User-Friendly

Now that you've learned how to **automate tasks in Excel**, it's time to make your macros more **interactive and user-friendly**. A good macro should not only run efficiently but also provide **clear feedback, accept user input, and be easy to execute**.

In this chapter, you'll learn how to:

✓ **Add message boxes for user interaction** – Display alerts and confirmations.

✓ **Use InputBoxes to collect user data** – Allow users to enter values dynamically.

✓ **Customize buttons to trigger macros easily** – Run macros with a single click.

By the end of this chapter, you'll be able to create **professional-looking macros that interact with users seamlessly!**

Adding message boxes for user interaction

What is a Message Box?

A **message box (MsgBox)** is a simple pop-up window that displays information or asks for user confirmation. It makes macros more interactive by providing **alerts, instructions, and error messages**.

VBA Code: Display a Simple Message Box

```
Sub ShowMessage()
    MsgBox "Hello! This is a VBA message box.",
vbInformation, "Welcome"
End Sub
```

Message Box Components:

✓ "Hello! This is a VBA message box." → The message displayed.
✓ vbInformation → Displays an **info icon**.
✓ "Welcome" → The title of the message box.

Try running the macro (F5) to see the message box appear!

Using Different Message Box Buttons

You can customize **buttons** to allow user choices:

VBA Constant	Description	Example
vbOKOnly	Shows only an OK button	MsgBox "Operation complete", vbOKOnly, "Info"
vbYesNo	Displays Yes and No buttons	MsgBox "Do you want to continue?", vbYesNo, "Confirm"
vbYesNoCancel	Shows Yes, No, and Cancel buttons	MsgBox "Save changes?", vbYesNoCancel, "Save"

VBA Code: Message Box with User Response

```vba
Sub ConfirmAction()
    Dim Response As Integer
    Response = MsgBox("Do you want to proceed?", vbYesNo,
"Confirmation")

    If Response = vbYes Then
        MsgBox "You clicked YES!", vbInformation,
"Confirmed"
    Else
        MsgBox "You clicked NO!", vbExclamation,
"Cancelled"
    End If
End Sub
```

This macro **asks for user confirmation** before proceeding with an action!

Using InputBoxes to collect user data

What is an InputBox?

An **InputBox** allows users to **enter data manually** while running a macro. This is useful when you need a **custom input like a name, number, or range selection**.

VBA Code: Get User Input and Display It

```
Sub GetUserName()

    Dim UserName As String

    UserName = InputBox("Enter your name:", "User Input")


    If UserName <> "" Then

        MsgBox "Hello, " & UserName & "!", vbInformation,
"Welcome"

    Else

        MsgBox "No name entered.", vbExclamation, "Error"

    End If

End Sub
```

How This Works:

✓ **Asks for the user's name.**
✓ **Displays a welcome message** if a name is entered.
✓ **Shows an error message** if the user leaves it blank.

 Try running this macro and entering your name!

Using InputBox for Numeric Input

You can also collect **numbers** and perform calculations.

```
Sub CalculateBonus()

    Dim Sales As Double

    Sales = InputBox("Enter sales amount:", "Sales Input")


    If IsNumeric(Sales) And Sales > 0 Then
```

```vba
    MsgBox "Your bonus is $" & Sales * 0.1,
vbInformation, "Bonus Calculation"
    Else
        MsgBox "Invalid input! Please enter a valid sales
amount.", vbCritical, "Error"
    End If
End Sub
```

This macro **calculates a 10% bonus** based on the user's sales input!

Using InputBox for Range Selection

Sometimes, you need the user to **select a range of cells** before running a macro.

```vba
Sub SelectRange()
    Dim UserRange As Range
    Set UserRange = Application.InputBox("Select a
range:", Type:=8)

    If Not UserRange Is Nothing Then
        MsgBox "You selected: " & UserRange.Address,
vbInformation, "Selection Confirmed"
    Else
        MsgBox "No range selected.", vbExclamation,
"Error"
    End If
End Sub
```

This macro allows users to **click and select a range**, then confirms their selection.

Customizing buttons to trigger macros easily

Why Use Buttons?

Instead of opening the VBA Editor every time, **adding buttons to your sheet** makes it **easy to run macros with a single click**.

How to Add a Button in Excel to Run a Macro

1□. Go to the **Developer Tab** → Click **Insert**.
2□. Under **Form Controls**, select **Button (Form Control)**.
3□. Click anywhere on the sheet to create a button.
4□. In the pop-up window, **assign a macro** (e.g., ShowMessage).
5□. Click **OK** – The button is now linked to your macro!

Click the button, and your macro runs instantly!

Creating a VBA Button Programmatically

You can also create a button **with VBA itself!**

```
Sub CreateButton()
    Dim btn As Object
    Set btn = ActiveSheet.Buttons.Add(100, 100, 100, 30) '
(Left, Top, Width, Height)
    btn.OnAction = "ShowMessage"
    btn.Caption = "Click Me!"
    btn.Font.Size = 12
End Sub
```

Run this macro, and it will create a button dynamically!

Final Thoughts: Your Macros Are Now Interactive!

Key Takeaways from This Chapter:

Message Boxes (MsgBox) provide alerts, confirmations, and instructions.

InputBoxes (InputBox) allow users to enter data dynamically.
Buttons make macros easy to run without opening the VBA Editor.

You've now built user-friendly macros that interact with users!

Next up: Debugging and Error Handling – Fixing Issues in Your Macros!

Chapter 7: Debugging and Error Handling Like a Pro

Even the best programmers make mistakes, and **debugging** is a critical skill in VBA. Whether it's a **syntax error, runtime error, or logical error**, knowing how to **identify and fix issues efficiently** will make your macros more reliable.

In this chapter, we'll cover:
✓ **Common VBA mistakes and how to fix them** – Learn the most frequent errors and their solutions.
✓ **Using breakpoints to pause and inspect code** – Debug like a pro with built-in VBA tools.
✓ **Best practices for writing clean and efficient VBA code** – Keep your macros optimized and error-free.

By the end of this chapter, you'll be able to **identify errors, debug effectively, and write robust VBA code that runs smoothly!**

Common VBA mistakes and how to fix them

1. Syntax Errors (Typos & Incorrect Commands)

What happens?
Excel highlights incorrect VBA code in **red** because it doesn't follow VBA rules.

Example: Forgetting closing quotes in MsgBox
Incorrect:

```
MsgBox "Hello
```

Correct:

```
MsgBox "Hello"
```

Example: Using an undefined variable
Incorrect:

```
MyNumber = 10   ' No variable declaration
```

Correct:

```
Dim MyNumber As Integer
MyNumber = 10
```

Fix: Always declare variables using Dim and check for typos!

---

2. Runtime Errors (Crashes While Running Macros)

What happens?
The macro starts but **stops unexpectedly** due to an error (e.g., dividing by zero, missing objects).

Example: Dividing by zero (Error 11: Division by zero)
Incorrect:

```
Dim result As Double
result = 100 / 0   ' Causes error!
```

Fix using **error handling**:

```
On Error Resume Next
Dim result As Double
```

```
result = 100 / 0
If Err.Number <> 0 Then MsgBox "Error: Division by zero!"
On Error GoTo 0
```

Fix: Use On Error Resume Next to handle runtime errors gracefully.

---

3. Logical Errors (Wrong Output Without Errors)

What happens?
Your macro runs but **gives incorrect results** (e.g., miscalculations, missing loops).

Example: Incorrect Loop Condition
Incorrect:

```
Dim i As Integer
For i = 1 To 10
    MsgBox i
    i = i + 1  ' This skips numbers!
Next i
```

Correct:

```
Dim i As Integer
For i = 1 To 10
    MsgBox i
Next i
```

Fix: Carefully check loop conditions and variable changes!

Using breakpoints to pause and inspect code

What Are Breakpoints?

Breakpoints **pause your code at a specific line**, allowing you to inspect variables, step through code, and find errors before they crash your macro.

How to Add a Breakpoint in VBA:

1. Open the **VBA Editor (ALT + F11)**.

2. Click inside a macro where you want to pause execution.

3. Press **F9**, or click **Debug > Toggle Breakpoint**.

4. When you run the macro, execution will **pause at the breakpoint**.

Example: Adding a Breakpoint in a Loop

```
Sub DebugExample()
    Dim i As Integer
    For i = 1 To 5
        Debug.Print "Iteration: " & i  ' Check values in
Immediate Window
    Next i
End Sub
```

Run the macro with **F5**, and execution will pause where you set a breakpoint!

Using the Immediate Window for Real-Time Debugging

The **Immediate Window** allows you to test VBA code and check variable values **while the macro is running**.

How to Open the Immediate Window:

1. Open **VBA Editor (ALT + F11)**.

2. Click **View > Immediate Window** (Ctrl + G).

3. Type the following command and press Enter:

```
? Range("A1").Value
```

4. The **current value of A1** will be displayed instantly!

Use ? VariableName to inspect values while debugging.

Best practices for writing clean and efficient VBA code

1. Always Declare Variables (Use Option Explicit)

Before writing VBA code, add **Option Explicit** at the top of your module:

```
Option Explicit
Dim Sales As Double
```

This forces you to declare all variables, preventing typos and unexpected errors.

---

2. Avoid Selecting Cells Unnecessarily

Inefficient Code:

```
Range("A1").Select
Selection.Value = "Hello"
```

Better Approach:

```
Range("A1").Value = "Hello"
```

Why? Selecting cells **slows down macros** unnecessarily.

---

3. Use Error Handling to Prevent Crashes

Instead of letting errors stop your macro, **use structured error handling**:

```
On Error GoTo ErrorHandler
Dim x As Integer
x = 10 / 0   ' This will cause an error!


Exit Sub  ' Prevents the error handler from running
unnecessarily.


ErrorHandler:
```

```
MsgBox "An error occurred: " & Err.Description
```

Your macro will now display an error message instead of crashing.

---

4. Write Modular Code (Use Subroutines and Functions)

Instead of writing one **long macro**, break it into **smaller, reusable subroutines**.

Messy, long code:

```
Sub ReportGenerator()
    ' Code to clean data
    ' Code to generate chart
    ' Code to email report
End Sub
```

Better approach (modular subroutines):

```
Sub CleanData()
    ' Data cleanup code here
End Sub


Sub GenerateChart()
    ' Chart creation code here
End Sub


Sub EmailReport()
    ' Email automation code here
End Sub


Sub ReportGenerator()
    CleanData
    GenerateChart
    EmailReport
End Sub
```

Why?

✓ Easier to **debug** each part separately.

✓ Can **reuse** subroutines in different macros.

---

5. Optimize Performance by Turning Off Screen Updating

If your macro processes large datasets, it can **run much faster** by disabling screen updates.

```
Sub FastMacro()
    Application.ScreenUpdating = False   ' Turn off screen
refresh
    Application.Calculation = xlCalculationManual   ' Turn
off auto-calculation

    ' Your macro code here

    Application.ScreenUpdating = True   ' Turn back on
    Application.Calculation = xlCalculationAutomatic   '
Restore calculation
End Sub
```

This can make macros up to 10x faster!

Final Thoughts: Debug Like a Pro!

Key Takeaways from This Chapter:

Common VBA mistakes include syntax errors, runtime errors, and logical errors.

Breakpoints (F9) pause your macro so you can inspect code step by step.

Use the Immediate Window (Ctrl + G) to test values while debugging.

Write clean VBA code with Option Explicit, modular subroutines, and optimized performance settings.

You now have the tools to troubleshoot, debug, and optimize your VBA macros like a pro!

Next up: Real-World VBA Projects – Bringing It All Together!

Chapter 8: Putting It All Together – Real-World Mini Projects

Now that you've learned the fundamentals of **VBA programming, automation, and debugging**, it's time to **apply everything to real-world mini projects**. These projects will help you **automate daily Excel tasks**, boost productivity, and solidify your understanding of VBA.

In this chapter, you'll build:

✓ **A weekly sales report automation** – Generate and format reports with one click.

✓ **A one-click data cleanup tool** – Fix messy data instantly.

✓ **A simple task tracker with VBA** – Track progress dynamically.

✓ **A roadmap for continuing your VBA learning** – Take your skills to the next level.

By the end of this chapter, you'll have built **practical VBA projects** that you can use in real work scenarios!

Automating a weekly sales report

Problem: Manually Creating Reports Every Week

Every week, sales managers spend time **copying, pasting, and formatting** sales data into a report. This process is slow and prone to human errors.

Solution: A VBA Macro to Generate Reports Automatically

This macro will:
✓ Copy sales data into a new sheet.
✓ Format headers and apply borders.
✓ Create a summary of total sales.

VBA Code: Weekly Sales Report Macro

```
Sub GenerateSalesReport()
    Dim wsSource As Worksheet, wsReport As Worksheet
    Dim LastRow As Long


    ' Define source and target sheets
    Set wsSource = ThisWorkbook.Sheets("SalesData")
    Set wsReport = ThisWorkbook.Sheets.Add
    wsReport.Name = "Weekly Report"


    ' Find last row in SalesData
    LastRow = wsSource.Cells(Rows.Count, 1).End(xlUp).Row


    ' Copy data to new report sheet
    wsSource.Range("A1:D" & LastRow).Copy
    wsReport.Range("A1").PasteSpecial Paste:=xlPasteValues


    ' Format headers
    wsReport.Rows(1).Font.Bold = True
    wsReport.Rows(1).Interior.Color = RGB(255, 255, 0)
```

```vba
' Auto-fit columns
wsReport.Cells.EntireColumn.AutoFit

' Add total sales summary
wsReport.Range("F1").Value = "Total Sales"
wsReport.Range("F2").Formula = "=SUM(D2:D" & LastRow &
")"

' Cleanup
Application.CutCopyMode = False


MsgBox "Weekly Sales Report Generated!",
vbInformation, "Success"
End Sub
```

How to Use It:

1☐. Make sure your sales data is in a sheet called "SalesData".
2☐. Run the macro (F5 in the VBA Editor).
3☐. A new **Weekly Report** sheet will be created instantly!

No more manual report creation—this macro does it all!

Creating a one-click data cleanup tool

Problem: Messy Data with Extra Spaces and Duplicates

If you work with **imported or manually entered data**, it often contains **extra spaces, blank rows, or duplicates** that need to be cleaned before analysis.

Solution: A VBA Macro to Clean Data Automatically

This macro will:
✓ Remove **extra spaces** from text.
✓ Delete **blank rows**.
✓ Remove **duplicate values**.

VBA Code: One-Click Data Cleaner

```
Sub CleanData()
    Dim ws As Worksheet
    Dim LastRow As Long, i As Long

    Set ws = ActiveSheet
    LastRow = ws.Cells(Rows.Count, 1).End(xlUp).Row

    ' Trim spaces in column A
    For i = 2 To LastRow
        ws.Cells(i, 1).Value = Trim(ws.Cells(i, 1).Value)
    Next i

    ' Remove blank rows
    For i = LastRow To 2 Step -1
        If WorksheetFunction.CountA(ws.Rows(i)) = 0 Then
            ws.Rows(i).Delete
        End If
    Next i

    ' Remove duplicates
```

```
    ws.Range("A1:A" & LastRow).RemoveDuplicates
Columns:=1, Header:=xlYes


    MsgBox "Data cleanup completed!", vbInformation,
"Success"
End Sub
```

How to Use It:

1□. Select the sheet containing messy data.
2□. Run the macro (F5 in the VBA Editor).
3□. Your data will be **cleaned automatically**—no manual editing needed!

This tool saves hours of manual data cleaning!

Setting up a simple task tracker with VBA

Problem: No Easy Way to Track Task Progress

Project managers and professionals often **manually update** task statuses in Excel, which can be slow and disorganized.

Solution: A VBA Macro to Track and Update Tasks

This macro will:
✓ Assign tasks **dynamically**.
✓ Update **task status** automatically.
✓ Highlight **completed tasks** for better visibility.

VBA Code: Task Tracker

```
Sub UpdateTaskStatus()
    Dim ws As Worksheet
    Dim LastRow As Long, i As Long

    Set ws = ThisWorkbook.Sheets("Tasks")
    LastRow = ws.Cells(Rows.Count, 1).End(xlUp).Row

    ' Loop through tasks
    For i = 2 To LastRow
        Select Case ws.Cells(i, 2).Value
            Case "Completed"
                ws.Cells(i, 1).Font.Strikethrough = True
                ws.Cells(i, 1).Interior.Color = RGB(144,
238, 144) ' Light green
            Case "In Progress"
                ws.Cells(i, 1).Interior.Color = RGB(255,
255, 153) ' Light yellow
            Case "Pending"
```

```
        ws.Cells(i, 1).Interior.Color = RGB(255,
153, 153) ' Light red
        End Select
    Next i


    MsgBox "Task statuses updated!", vbInformation,
"Success"
End Sub
```

How to Use It:

1☐. Create a **"Tasks"** sheet with tasks in column A and their **status** in column B (Completed, In Progress, or Pending).

2☐. Run the macro (F5 in the VBA Editor).

3☐. The macro **highlights completed tasks in green, in-progress tasks in yellow, and pending tasks in red!**

No more manually tracking tasks—VBA does it instantly!

Next steps: How to continue learning VBA

1. Explore More Advanced VBA Topics

Now that you know the basics, here are some **next-level VBA skills** to master:

✓ **UserForms** – Create interactive input forms.

✓ **Working with External Data** – Connect Excel to databases.

✓ **VBA for Outlook & Word** – Automate emails and documents.

---

2. Join Online VBA Communities

To keep improving, join VBA learning communities:

◆ **Stack Overflow** – Ask and answer VBA-related questions.

◆ **Microsoft Learn** – Official VBA documentation.

◆ **Reddit & LinkedIn Groups** – Connect with Excel automation experts.

---

3. Automate Real-World Excel Tasks

Start applying VBA to your **daily Excel work**:
Automate **data entry & formatting**
Build **interactive dashboards**
Create **customized Excel add-ins**

The more you practice, the more confident you'll become in **writing VBA macros that save time and improve efficiency**!

Final Thoughts: You Are Now a VBA Automation Expert!

Key Takeaways from This Chapter:

Automate weekly reports to save hours of work.

Create a one-click data cleanup tool for fast and error-free data handling.

Build a task tracker that updates statuses automatically.

Continue learning VBA by exploring advanced topics and real-world applications.

You are now equipped with the skills to automate Excel and boost productivity!

Next up: Expanding Your VBA Skills – Advanced Topics and Real-World Applications!

More books about VBA&macro you can find here
https://kdp.amazon.com/en_US/series/PT199GD4HAV

or, if you prefer QR code, here

www.ingramcontent.com/pod-product-compliance
Lightning Source LLC
Chambersburg PA
CBHW071030050326
40689CB00014B/3594